D1605654

Whiskey, X-Ray, Yankee

Dara-Lyn Shrager

Barrow Street Press
New York City

Designed by Mollie Bergeron
Cover design by Rachel Marie Patterson
Author photo by Laura Pedrick
Cover art: "Me upon My Pony on My Boat"
        by Chris Roberts-Antieau

Published 2018 by Barrow Street, Inc., a not-for-profit
(501) (c) (3) corporation. All contributions are tax deductible.
Distributed by:
        Barrow Street Books
        P.O. Box 1558
        Kingston, RI 02881

Barrow Street Books are also distributed by Small Press
Distribution, SPD, 1341 Seventh Street Berkeley, CA 94710-
1409, spd@spdbooks.org; (510) 524-1668, (800) 869-7553
(Toll-free within the US); amazon.com; Ingram Periodicals,
Inc., 1240 Heil Quaker Blvd, PO Box 7000, La Vergne, TN
37086-700 (615) 213-3573; and Armadillo & Co., 7310 S. La
Cienega Blvd, Inglewood, CA 90302, (310) 693-6061.

First Edition

Library of Congress Control Number: 2018930635

ISBN 978-0-9997461-4-1

Whiskey, X-Ray, Yankee

For Danny

CONTENTS

Traps

Because it seems the day begins
when it begins for me, this deer
must be only moments dead. See
its wet, raw rump blooming
in the grass, so new to this ridge
by the side of the road that crows
have yet to chatter over its body,
to figure a way in. The meat will
still be warm. Pulling the latch
on his cargo bed, the man makes
room among the catch poles, cages,
tongs, and traps for his morning's
first collection—a specimen of
near perfection—dragged then
dumped by the morning rush.

Crown of Thorns

I held him through that first sea storm,
my newborn son, his body moving in womb
memory. Tonight, I see him for the first
time since then; the waves have changed
his face. There are 1800 species of sea stars,
but only one crown of thorns, cloaked in spines
that pierce the skin. When my son stings,
my wounds bloom dark roses in the water.
When I fan out my arms to forgive him,
he swims on, into the black mouth of the reef.

Bloodless Daughter

What peril blooms
inside like mushrooms
I will not see until I wake
to find it spotting my lawn,
poisoning the dog.

I could also wake to find
wild flowers uncurling
their petals in a wave
of violet spray.

Morning Song

He pecks me awake before the hills
have rolled out their green tongues.
This is why I love the woodpecker best
of all the birds in our double-woods.
(It is easy to love the woodpecker best
if you are sewn to your days as I am
sewn to mine.) He does not spy a tree
and ask the universe a question. No.
For him, there is no doubt.

The Club

The women eat egg salad sandwiches.
Baby redpolls leave their nests, feast
then tip to their deaths in wet tombs.
While the women are away scratching
their sailboat rudders against rocks,
engraving themselves on a tiny coast,
the moon-faced lady, inside whose chest
black poppies bloom, will loosen shags
of her own blonde curls. Her husband
will miss her tiny breasts. Her three
small sons will try to push their wooden
trains under her bathroom door.

Under

I see him go under. His hair
the color of cinder, spraying out
from his scalp as he sinks, the dead
leg heavy as a tomb. Down to the tiles
slick with black mold. To the static
place underwater where voices sound
like muted horns and the treetops smear.
He cannot pull himself from the pool
so his club sandwich sours in the sun,
on a metal dining table rusting
at the joints. Wasps nest in their mud
cones, stuck to the underside of every
chair in which he can no longer sit.
On the courts near the water where he
cannot float, white skirts swish
and tennis balls arc through the sky.

What Another Mother

Yes, she laid her
spine in the silt, in
the rain-suck-swirl
by the reservoir, in
the cold that pickled her
fingertips. Her hair
spun a nest of twigs
and clay where she lay,
in a space so narrow
no coffee-maker or ringing
phone could be wedged
in. A hollow where she
used to be. I keep telling
the punch-drunk townies
that I never knew her,
but oh—

Setting the Table

Nights, I bruise my knees
while Mother aches, pinned to floral
sheets, my small hand reaching up,
her cool hand hanging down.
She cooks nothing now
the map of her is torn in half.
Where she used to sit, an empty
chair at the four-square table
by the long, white electric cord.
No more lidded bowls of hot, white rice,
no flattened breasts of chicken
pounded down. I don't forgive her.

Before

The dog is not with me anymore.
I hauled her in a cardboard box
into a room so sterile
that the bleached air stung.
Green bottles of antiseptic glowed electric.
Towels stiff with hospital soap hung by.
Her body was leaking onto the metal table
and the scrub-tired linoleum floor.
When she split open,
a distance widened between us.
She was not mine anymore
and I was not mine either.

Seagull

This one, whose call I know,
is backwards and flat to the road,
black-billed, white-bellied,
brown and pewter feathers clasped.
If I ride back in a week, this bird's body
will have sunk into the street,
a flung rag, gut-stuck,
nothing anyone in a car might see—
that loud metal box
a mean machine.

Hand-Sewn

My boys love damp October days,
the chilled air stamping their faces,
crescents of dew on their sneakers.
One is telling me something about gym
and how the teacher makes them run.
The sun throws shards of light across
the near side of his face where sweat
has salted tiny hairs white. Now the memory
of that scorched hour—the gloved hands
cupping his chin, the silver hook lacing
the flesh over his left eye. Between him
and the sharpest edges there is only this:
a fine veneer of epithelial cells, some keratin.

View from the Leeward Deck

We spent my lifetime scooping water back into the sea
with half-gallon jugs relieved of their mouths, buckets lacking
handles, yellow rain boots, our puckered hands. Cold, green
waves muscled their way aboard and began to swallow
the fiberglass hull keeping us from the pitch & dumb
of the black sea floor. While you were wrestling the snapping jib,

I simply floated away. A plastic spoon in a wide, china bowl.

Now you are sailing far from the cove's dark embrace.
You don't see me but I'm back with you, worrying over sand bars
and whitecaps. Salt-blind, you man the tiller, cursing lanterns
that have burned through the last of their kerosene. My father,
you are as near to broken as your ship of splintered teak and chafing
hull. And I am the halyards, clanging all through the night in song.

Who Left You Beside the Road

Who left you beside the road with your neck
unhinged? So close to you, I am afraid your body
will find its figure again and rush
toward me in a white bolt or away like a fawn,
cracking through the brush.

(When we were children, he stood
on his well-made bed and sang La Traviata.
Fat boy in scratchy socks and hard black shoes,
the boom of his voice smothered me.)

I think that now your belly
is softening. If I turn you over,
there will be beetles soldiering through.
Your feet will take you nowhere softly.
Brother, you should know the war
is over. I am not angry anymore.

Who Knew Their Feathers Shine Like Mink

Who dies with its eyes open,
its wing bones splayed.
I could step over it. This is not
my town. The dead are not
my own. But I stop for nearly
an hour, an autopsy with a stick,
a half-prayer, a few kind words
about birds in general,
but especially crows. Who knew
their feathers shine like mink?
Dark eyes, black bill, black
talons curled on black feet.
Regal pavement raven, now
so close it's nearly violet-black
in the soft, damp cup of my hands.
Mother left when I was nine,
floated over my pink wicker bed
in her white flannel nightgown
on the longest nights of the year.
How the wind smacked
my windows like a pair of wings.
How should death go?
I have only a sandwich wrapper
for a shroud. Who will wear
these feathers now
I wear my mother's clothes?

Keep

Black are his burial shoes and his daughter's hair.
His wife is as faint as the sky digging crudely at
their backs. There must be more than just cars
bumping by, squares of dirt, severed tangle of winter
weeds. Somebody bring these ladies inside, see how
they hold the steam sailing from the mouths of two
painted cups so close to their disappearing faces.

With a Diamond Knife

No escaping the pinch
and rapture of living.
Across my back, a jagged row
of rotten teeth clenched shut.
I had caught the sun
in the melanin of my skin.
Now nothing left but truant cells
floating lazily in formalin.
But I was here,
stopped mid-death,
dripping pitch like honey
from the cleaved hive.

I Go Like This

Somebody with ill intentions has come to my door.
When he knocks, a murder of crows ascends
from the roof like a hat lifting from a mourner's head.
Don't we all believe ourselves exempt until we're suddenly—
or slowly (with needles) not?

Two raps on the wood. A formality, as it turns out.

He moves along the inside of our bodies like paper
in flames. If I hide in my closet, he wears me there too.
When he offers his hand, I have already locked fingers
with him. Even if I thrash and call out for my mother
like a child, he'll note my tongue and add it to the list
of parts he'll take. In a basket I will go, my house
whipped clean of cutlery and bones.

Incantation

The voice on the line wants me to know
that we're not alone—the same rib made her
as made me. There are other operators
in the room; I hear them pricing minivans.
Now she is asking me to pray. What I want
to say: just today, I watched a thousand
dandelion flowers brush sideways across
the flattest, greenest leaves I've ever seen.
Irene.
Irene.

Still

In this picture, I hold my baby
like a bouquet. His doughy joy
softens the entire frame. He
makes me pretty where I am not,
and I worry that this is why
I love him. My older boy clowns
his green eyes wide and the baby
laughs, leaning toward his brother
like a stalk seeking sun.
I wear my skin tight and the children
look right. What the days will develop
into I cannot know, here, captured
long before cells divided me down.

The Corners of His Lips

At first, it seems a heap of fronds, a pile
of clothes. Bound in fishing line, knotted
up, its slate feathers drying in the sun, pouch
empty. Boy lifts the tangled line and with it
the pelican's head. Up and down he throws
the seabird's bill. We are standing so far apart,
I cannot see which way the corners of his lips
turn. He pulls the bird like a dog, which it is not.
It isn't even a bird anymore.

Schneider's Skink

The skink is hollow now—
two years of life seeping
into the sand,
spiking the air.
Boy blames himself,
the cricket-giver, water-changer,
for letting the taper-tailed reptile
slip soundlessly from us
inside her glass dome.
What can we say?
The skink lived well,
burrowed, hunted, cooled
her overlapping, burnished scales
in a shallow rock pool.
We load the whole tragic theater
to the top of a ravine and dump it
down to be swallowed
by the teeming marsh.
By daybreak, silver-haired bats
will have taken her.

Whiskey, X-Ray, Yankee

When the dinghy engine failed to start, I tied
a thousand figure eights and my fingers pruned.
The brackish waters were boozy with gasoline.
That night, a plastic moon above the main hatch
and the propane stink of a gimbaled stove, while
the bilge pump choked in the fiberglass hull. Slaps
enough from the green sea. The rest of the family
slept because they could in moldy bunks, black
confetti on white vinyl, the teak weathered gray.
I camped by the CB calling *Whiskey, X-Ray, Yankee,*
9-1-8-0. The stars looked dry and too distant
to care. At daybreak I woke on the aft deck
soaked in dew, mildew creeping along the inside
of my back. I have smelled it inside my nose
for years. I have gotten so good at forgiving.

Babysitting Money

I steal records. 45s.
I have babysitting money.
It isn't about what I can't afford.
I hang around the mall throwing pennies.
If I rub my head with the neon yellow
bag, my hair stands up.

At school, I pay Nancy Hull to sneak
stickers from the Teacher's closet
and stick them on my closet door.
My mother asks me where
I get them—and exactly when
and how. Babysitting money,
I say to her face.

I mind the neighbors after school.
One time, the baby rolled off
the changing table. Her naked body
bounced on the carpet, and her tongue
went blue before she cried.

I am ten. Dirty girl, I think I hear
in rooms I'm drifting through.

Shasta Road

Someone sliced two carpet squares
and tossed them underneath
the swings. That summer, the scent
of roses was so heady, fat bees
fell recklessly to sleep. After rain,
mud sucked the swing set poles
out of the deep holes meant
to hold them. And the worms,
the weeds, the lit sticks of punk
we waved to keep mosquitos
away. How it all must have looked
to a stranger circling the block
in his brown sedan.
Blame the horn he blared,
the rocks we threw, the swift
chase, the ropey arms tossing
Nancy into the back of his car.
Blame the sharpened blade.

Monkey

The little stuffed monkey wore underpants
and somebody named him before she named
me. It wasn't his fault that the monkey
came first. My mother cooked roasts
and my father carved them with a silver, electric
knife. Fancy pan. Stucco house. Angry brother
with the one-eyed monkey on his well-made bed.

Firstborn

I writhe. I nearly drown.
On the second day, I stop hearing
words, only my blood sluicing.
On the third, I split and multiply.
Boy arrives nearly spent,
a map crumpled in his blue hands.
I hold it to my heart, my eyes, my eyes,
my lips as I lean toward his fretted brow.
He is more anguished than pleased
by the light. But I am not
his wretched keeper nor is he mine.
We have only left our private islands.
There is nothing to do but swim
so we swim toward each other.

The Breathers

Boy tells me they enter at night
and crouch in closets wheezing.
It's true we hear them from our beds.
Then I see them in the waiting room
under pulpy copies of *Highlights*.
They perch on tiny chairs cut
from foam. The doctors call
for vials of Boy's bad blood
but he isn't giving any away.
No one here can open himself
even wide enough for a pin.
The Breathers wait in every
corner of the Big Fear Box.

Muck, Fallen Trees, Fire

A baby born underwater
doesn't reach for air,
he fans out his silver fingers
and swims. A city heaving grief
crawls away from breathless birds.
One man dies with a hammer
in hand, hooked to his roof
by the pick end, a jagged slice
of sky in his milky eyes.
The best advice we get:
tie the dead to telephone poles
and set their souls on unhinged doors.

A Moment Alone

She opened her hands
and fogged the air
with a fine talcum.
Weightless she was
and without words.
It wasn't the worst
of her days; the bowl
of the earth warmed
the pads of her feet, and
the future—it could still be
like a story, crowded
with braided oval rugs
and crystal goblets
bending light. She stripped
herself and waited,
mute as the mail slot.

Retreat

Against black winds cutting in from Rocky Mountain,
six cows in a shed shift their feet. I follow the scrape
of hooves until I find their heat. Anything to escape
where I have come to know myself awfully
and without error, my pulse set to the kettle's wail,
a single track wearing grooves in my head—
three of the broads are bloated with calves,
one so laden she turns away and eases
her haunches into the sorghum hay—
soggy, word-bitten, tired in the eyes from seeing.

Years In

I let that clip run on a loop,
always watching your white face
flashing, the undulations of your flesh,
speed thinning you out as you go,
a kingfisher diving into asphalt,
or maybe just a human body
doing terrible things with gravity.
If I could turn you off before
you land, I always would.

Red Moon

This is how we find them,
marking the ground we travel,
hundreds of monarch butterflies
among asphalt pebbles, flattened
beer cans, shreds of newsprint,
cigarette thumbs. There is no end
to the dead; they multiply
like wing beats. The truth is:
this warm September day
is beautiful and plain.

Robin II

Plump robin on the bluestone
steps where mint crawls. I raked
you into the wild plants. I murdered
what was already dead, then waited
on the rain and heat to swallow
you in. Funny how the hungry
hound never smells you there.

Son in Sleep

Yesterday, your Appaloosa colt
stepped into a mob of bees and bolted
for the heavy brush. Half-blind, you
followed me back down the ridge.
At the ranch, I showed you a tiny bottle
of equine eye drops, begged you to blink
them in—no help within a half-day's drive
and the sun suddenly seeming so cold.
We were all kneeling down,
and I held that cloudy vessel of you.

Shelter in Place

They did. All day. In the basement where the janitor sips
coffee in a metal cage, where buttons blink red and mops
stand like flamingos, where grey machines hum breath
into this building. Some of the girls sit cross-legged
on the cement floor, tapping at phones with no service,
asking each other questions. Their voices are high and thin.
When it's over, they pack their books, shrug racquet bags
onto their shoulders and make their way to the fields.
Under this weight, their bodies hunch forward and tip
to one side. Parked where I watch the procession, scanning
for the one face that translates to meaning for me, I notice,
on just this day, how thin the skin on my boy's face looks,
how much like the shell of an egg, and how open
it can suddenly become. By bullet, by bomb, by hand.

Beth Israel

The baby arrived with legs
that swung out like doors set
backwards on their hinges.
Across from the building where
he was born, another building
to tell us *he will walk*
or *no*. So we went, wrapped
in scarves against the sideways
snow. Just one day after that
blue coil sprung away from him
then back, dropping onto my belly
with a wet thud. And the red
river pooling in the shallows
where the floor was worn,
painting the soles of white clogs
dancing all around my hospital
bed. I did not feel the pouring
but I imagined I could. That next
day, faces stamped blank. We rode
the escalator that swallowed
its own silver teeth. If you have ever
stolen anything then you know how
we left that place, hunched over
our new possession, eyes down,
mouths tight, ready to sprint
if anyone called our names.

Devotional

The black woolly caterpillar predicted
a long, harsh winter, and it came. Now
it's April. Flying ants dive-bomb the deck
and frantic bees build hive cones
in the high joints of the house's frame.
When my son left, I hung his pirate robe
in the closet next to mine. Out in the yard,
his old lacrosse net waves its frayed flags
at the sudden spring. And just beside it,
the caterpillar, dead, a stinging inch of shiny
bristles. Whose body lasted through winter,
unwithered. All this must mean something.

Bee Mountain

We wake. We burn in a ring
of trees. In a high call, they sing.
The sun finds us and slips
us on like a strand of hot metal beads.
When our bones upturn in the soft
earth, seasons later, count us
among the mountain's unwelcome.

Single Farmer

I was dreaming so I didn't hear you go
but wheel tracks have hardened on
the muddy field. Did you stop
even once and lay the reins across your lap,
thinking it might be easier to come back,
brew a pot of coffee, fry some eggs,
holler to me the hens are fed?
The only thing this farm has taught me
beats against the window like a storm.
It's not what people say that kills,
or the empty root cellar in winter.
Just these panes holding nothing but light.

Wild Child

When my mother's back broke like sticks,
the crows descended on our fields of corn
and the barn walls crumbled into hard-packed dirt.

I served her hot tea on a bed tray painted
with cabbage roses, then walked my flat, sour belly
to school and beat the front teeth out of Michael Lee.

I am nobody's friend and you can't make me.
It took my mother nine months to find her feet again.
The crops rotted on their stems and the mud storms
swallowed the barn's last legs and all the bad babies in.

The Second Secret

Two girls share a bike.
One pedals, steers, avoids potholes.
Two holds on to One's waist and
speaks too hotly in One's ear.

At the park, they see a man
open his coat. One pedals home.
Two slides off the seat crying.
A police car rides them back down.
Either they are lying or the man is gone.

One doesn't know the truth.
She is the kind of girl who lets things happen.
Two takes off her pants in the metal shed.
Come closer, she says to One at the door.

The Hedge

The book of secrets opened when
the copper-haired girl approached
a rose hedge in bloom, reached
for a handful of thick perfume, and bled.
When she wiped her pierced fingertip
on her sleeve—white corduroy printed
with tiny strawberries—her blood
connected the berries by their stems.
She painted like this for a while.

Gardiner House

All the girls had spoons, bent to mimic the curves
of their throats. All the girls ate cake. Like swans.
With their long spines telescoping toward the purple
icing. The bathroom pipes chattered. Their bodies
swung on hinges. They painted their fingernails
red before palming themselves into bed, working
the white quilts to their chins. Saturday nights
they smoothed their hair in plaits over ghost ladders
of burns. Their robes billowed as they flew
the central stairway, up and down. No matter
the weather, the doors on that whitewashed Federal

                                                  stuck shut.

Grasp

My body is a ship housing three hammocks
in a swaying cabin: one for the heart, one
for the womb, one for the head. The middle
cradle has come untethered, hangs limply
from just one salt-sprayed hook. I dreamt
the baby a hundred times before we buried her
body next to Circuit City. We use a map
to find her: row 21, plot 63. Without a home,
sorrow bangs up against the heart hammock.
The baby left through the pierce in my ear,
the only place I could not hold her in.

Moon Rock

The last of the snow is a pocked, black moon rock
on the street that leads back to my son's door.
Inside a capsule bathed in artificial light, he was singing
a Jim Reeves song. Now I steer under a stone bridge,
traveling the curled lip of an entry ramp, shoved along
then hurtled when the road splits again.
The streetlights blink blurry and the horns lament.
New York is mostly rock. Why can't I forget the clock
and abandon the car when it comes to idle
at the toll plaza? The man in the booth says backing up
before I pay is a moving violation. How many more times
will I hear my son sing? Night drivers keen toward the city.
I am Jersey-bound for the millionth time. Plastic bags
float toward bare branches, some landing softly
like bubbles, some skewered and snapping. By now,
my boy might be sleeping. My car is just another bit
of space debris.

To See My Son Tour with the Band

This train is for Cork as am I,
for grey rock piles by the tracks
and cows curled on the knotty greens.
For mountains dusted in powdered light
when the rim of the sky peels back.
I am for Cork and my boy rattles
that way too, close by on a motorway
drawn into the portrait with a steady hand.
Little country with its painted doors
and polished brass, porcelain and broken
stone. This deep bowl of earth chipped
and teeming. For Cork, where I'll wait
on a quay with the rain in my face, the blue
doors smeared, the red ones slick
as autumn leaves choking the sewers shut.

The Dying Length

A man reads the letters Descartes wrote
to Pascal, then walks to the water's edge.
Better not to see the steel-blue surface
of everything. How cars whiz past, scraping
at the asphalt. How sharp mothers refuse
to meet the wet stares of children strapped
to car seats—little astronauts shuttling
nowhere fast. He lowers himself into the reeds,
where eiders nest in downy beds.

At Mason Family & Sons

He is more elegant than he ever was in life,
his morning-hair behaved, his skin bright
though lacking light, hands finally mute.
I've never pressed the clean half moons
at his fingertips. Behind me, the wooden chairs
creak as mourners shuffle their legs and clear
their throats. He was a difficult man. His eyelashes
are so long they curl against his cheeks.
I can make him any way I want. Everyone here
will understand. Their eyes flashed the ground
when I entered this room. Nobody wants the truth.

ACKNOWLEDGMENTS

Thank you to the following publications, in which some of these poems first appeared:

Barn Owl Review
Barnstorm Journal
Better Magazine
The Boiler Journal
Broadsided
District Lit
The Greensboro Review
Nashville Review
Orange Room Review
Passages North
Pebble Lake Review
Revolution House
Salamander
Southern Humanities Review
Thrush Poetry Journal
Tinderbox Poetry Journal
Verse Daily
Yemassee
Whiskey Island

 Dara-Lyn Shrager lives in Princeton, New Jersey, and is the co-founder and editor of *Radar Poetry*. She holds an MFA from Bennington College and a BA from Smith College. Her poems appear or are forthcoming in many journals, including *Southern Humanities Review*, *Barn Owl Review*, *Salamander*, *Yemassee*, *Whiskey Island*, *Tinderbox*, and *Nashville Review*. Her articles have appeared in newspapers and magazines including *The New York Times*, *The Philadelphia Inquirer*, and *Philadelphia Magazine*. Learn more at: www.daralynshrager.com.

BARROW STREET POETRY

We Step into the Sea: New and Selected Poems
Claudia Keelan (2018)

Luminous Debris: New & Selected Legerdemain 1992–2017
Timothy Liu (2018)

For the Fire from the Straw
Heidi Lynn Nilsson (2017)

Alma Almanac
Sarah Ann Winn (2017)

A Dangling House
Maeve Kinkead (2017)

Noon until Night
Richard Hoffman (2017)

Kingdom Come Radio Show
Joni Wallace (2016)

In Which I Play the Runway
Rochelle Hurt (2016)

Detainee
Miguel Murphy (2016)

Our Emotions Get Carried Away Beyond Us
Danielle Candena Deulen (2015)

Radioland
Lesley Wheeler (2015)

Tributary
Kevin McLellan (2015)

Horse Medicine
Doug Anderson (2015)

Unions
Alfred Corn (2014)

O, Heart
Claudia Keelan (2014)

Last Psalm at Sea Level
Meg Day (2014)

This Version of Earth
Soraya Shalforoosh (2014)

Vestigial
Page Hill Starzinger (2013)

You Have to Laugh: New + Selected Poems
Mairéad Byrne (2013)

Wreck Me
Sally Ball (2013)

Blight, Blight, Blight, Ray of Hope
Frank Montesonti (2012)

Self-evident
Scott Hightower (2012)

Emblem
Richard Hoffman (2011)

Mechanical Fireflies
Doug Ramspeck (2011)